Don't Be Stupid

5 Steps Any Idiot Can Do - Yes, Even You.

Silly Turtle Press

Silly Turtle Press

Table of Contents

Introduction

Let me guess - you didn't buy this book for yourself.

Did you?

A good friend or family member got it for you, right?

Yea, that's what I thought.

Right now I bet you are wondering, "Why would anybody give me this?"

Well, it's simple... *somebody thinks you're **stupid***.

I'm sorry that I have to be the one to break it to you, but I'm sure they're **right.**

What you should do now is thank that person; maybe even hug them or give them a big kiss, because if you take the time to read and **really** dig in and study this book, it will change your life!

You don't have to keep living this way; you don't *have* to be **stupid** forever, you *can* change!

The good news is someone cares about you enough to really want to help you! Right now is the time to accept that help; *embrace it*.

The best thing to do is face the fact that you're basically an *idiot* and just get it over with. Then start reading this informative book that will hopefully get you on the right track.

As someone who has worked with the public for over 30 years, I've been exposed to countless dumb-asses in my life. A large part of my career requires me to educate the public, which has made me an expert on what I call *Stupid Idiot Syndrome.*

Rest assured, I am going to guide you down the path to overcoming this dibilitating condition.

I am going to give you 5 steps that are *so easy* that **any** idiot can use them to overcome being a complete moron.

Don't put it off!

Start right now, because the sooner you do, the sooner you will be on your way to being someone who isn't a total **stooge**.

All you need to do is read the book and follow the instructions.

You'll have to stop here and there to think things over, but that is just part of the process. It might sound hard right now, but you really *can* do it if you just make the commitment.

I'm not saying it is going to be an effortless task, but if you stick with it, before you know it, you'll be getting a **lot** more respect and *perhaps* someday you will even be able to *identify someone else* who is stupid and needs this book too. Then you can do your part in helping society by passing it on.

Just remember, any idiot in the world can do it - even YOU!

I wish you the best of luck on your journey!

Step 1: Pull Your Head Out of Your Ass

I know - you don't think you're stupid and of course, you're unaware of the fact that your head is buried deep up there where the sun don't shine.

That's because it's *very hard* to think right with your head stuffed up your ass. The noxious fumes have turned your brain to mush!

Since I already *know* you're going to have a hard time with this, let me help you to see it for yourself.

Ask yourself these questions to know for yourself, *"Is my head up my ass?"*

1. When you are in your car, sitting at a red light, *how do you know when it is your turn to go? - Could* it be when you start hearing honking from the cars behind you?

2. Do you notice that other people are mostly rude and flip you off a lot? Do you get a lot of rude looks?

3. Are other people often *impatient* with you? Do you hear things like *"Excuse me!"* and *"Get out of the way!"* a lot?

4. Do *other* people seem to *always* be bumping into *you*?

5. Have you ever been nearly run over when crossing the road? *How many times would you say?*

6. As soon as the elevator door opens, do you *jump right in*? Do the people trying to *get out* get in *your* way? Do *they* give you rude looks **too**?

7. Are you *even aware* that there are other people on this planet besides **you**?

Ok! If you answered "yes" to 3 or more of those questions (*and be honest*), then you are indeed **stupid** and need to get your *head out of your ass*.

Now!

Yes, right now.

Reach down there and pull it out!

I'll wait - just stop here and **do it**.

———◄O►———

OK! *Doesn't that feel better?*

Take a couple of deep breaths of fresh air.

And – *Wipe the shit out of your eyes!*

Now that your head is out of your ass, the next thing you need to do is take a good look around.

Go ahead and start out looking straight ahead to see what is in front of you. Ok, now turn your head to the left to see what's beside you. After that, look over to the right to see what's over there. *Every now and then*, you're going to want to glance over your shoulder so you can be aware of what is behind you too.

(Pay attention here because this one little trick is going to help you eliminate about 50% of your problems.)

While you do this exercise ask yourself, "*Do I see anyone else? Am I alone, or are there other people around*?" This is called *being aware of other people*.

This exercise is something that you need to do a lot, especially when you leave your house. It doesn't matter if you are walking or driving in your truck, you *have **got** to* look around a lot to see what's out there besides yourself.

You *might* just realize that all that stuff happens to you because your **dumb ass** is *always* in the way.

I know you don't mean it.

Your head has just been buried up your **wazoo** and you *didn't know* anyone else was there. But now you do, so *you're going to have to do better from now on.*

Like when you are walking in a store or on a sidewalk, and you *just stop and stand* there – *probably* trying to remember what you were doing in the first place - your dumb ass is in everyone *else's* way! No worries; it's an easy fix. Just *move the hell over* so people can get by while you figure it out.

Here's another example: You may not be *trying* to piss everyone off by making a *right* turn from the **left** lane, but when your head was up your ass, you couldn't be bothered to notice the other cars on the road. Don't be the jackass who ran someone off the road because you forgot your exit. Just drive to the next one and turn around!

(I bet you think that there are a ton of bad drivers who can't even stay on the road – don't you?)

Seriously - what is actually going through your head when you're behind the wheel? *My guess is -* **nothing**!

The good news is, I am here to help end these problems for you!

Practice Thinking About Stuff

At this time, I am going to ask some questions. Don't just glance over this list and keep going. I want you to stop and think about each one before moving on to the next.

For this to work, you have to actually take a few minutes and think. Maybe try to see it in your head. I want you to see if you can come up with a logical answer for every question.

If you can't, it means that you are a self-absorbed asshat and really need to work on being aware of others!

- How do you expect anyone to get in or out if you are standing right in the middle of the doorway? (*Remember- try to picture it in your head) How would that work?*

- How can other drivers know that you're changing lanes if you don't put on a turn signal? Some people call it a blinker. (*In case you don't know what that is, take a minute to Google it!*)

- How can someone sit beside you on a plane or bus if *your* **elbows** are taking up half of the seat beside you?

- If you don't look both ways before walking across a road or parking lot, *how will you know if a car is coming or not*?

- Are you *always* lucky enough to be "*next*" - **OR** - *could* all those other people standing around, *one behind the other*, be waiting in line?

OK, that's enough questions for now. I don't want to overwork your pea brain, *after all*, it's not used to working this hard, is it?

How do you think you did? Let's review:

- If you are standing in the middle of the doorway, then no one can go in or out - *Go stand somewhere else!*

- No one knows where you're going if you don't use a turn signal. That's why they don't ever "let you over" when you are changing lanes – *Just use the damn thing!*

- Does the person sitting beside you seem a bit hostile? It's because they can't be comfortable trying to make room in *their* seat with *your* arms in the way - *Stay on your side!*

- Yes - you do have the right-of-way most of the time when you are walking – BUT you can be *correct* and *dead* at the same time if you step in front of a car - *All you have to do is turn your head and look before crossing!*

- Those people are **not** just hanging around because they have nothing better to do. - *Find the end of the line and wait there!*

Now that you've gotten a little practice thinking about stuff, you need to go out into the world and think about more stuff. This is really going to help you get better at not pissing people off all the time.

It's a good idea to think about what you are going to do before you actually do it. While you are thinking things over, consider this:

- Will other people be around? If so, what might they be doing?

- If you are going to stop or change directions, is it possible that some other person might be affected?

- Will there be other cars on the road?

- Will other people or things be within arms reach?

Just remember, you **will not always** be the *only* person there, so you need to plan for that.

If you are doing something and you notice that people seem to be giving you dirty looks (or worse), then move to a place where you will not block traffic and think about what you could have been doing to annoy everyone else.

Also, keep in mind that some people might just not be as friendly as you. They may want you to stand back a bit more than 4 inches from them. A good rule of thumb is to keep about 2 to 3 feet between you and other people, especially if you don't know them.

One more thing - when you're talking to somebody, it isn't *necessary* to lean in so close that they can smell your breath either. I *promise*, they don't mind the mystery of how bad your breath stinks, and you are *not obligated* to show it off to everyone!

Now that you have gotten some fresh air to that head of yours, and you've practiced thinking about things a bit, it's time to move on. In the next chapter, you are going to learn how to tell if you are right about something (*or if you're just being an idiot* as usual), and what to do when you find out that you are, in fact, wrong. This is where you are going to put all this "thinking" practice to good work.

Step 2: Admit You are Stupid

I am going to start this lesson by telling you about two scientists named David Dunning and Justin Kruger. These guys studied people for a long time.

Now, I'm not going to make this hard by trying to explain it all or using *fancy scientific language that you wouldn't understand*, so don't worry about that.

To sum it up, their research showed that stupid people *don't know* they are stupid; in fact, they are 100 percent sure they are *smart*. This makes them very confident that they are almost always right.

(Does that sound like anyone you know?)

This is called the "Dunning-Kruger Effect" and I would definitely say that you are most **certainly** one of those people.

Adam Robinson defined stupid as [quote] "*Overlooking or dismissing conspicuously crucial information.*" [quote]

What that means in simple terms is that you don't notice, or *you just ignore*, information that is necessary and right in front of you.

Think about this: how often do your friends say things like:

- Listen, dummy!

- It's not hard!

- *Can't you see it with your own eyes?*

- How are you **not** getting this?

- How **stupid** can you be?

- What part *don't* you understand?

You see, those are little clues. Your friends are trying to show you where you are wrong and the evidence is right before your eyes, but you can't seem to see it. Most likely if you do see it, you completely disregard it without even thinking that you could be wrong.

(There's that whole "thinking" thing again.)

What you need is to realize that you are not always right - you probably *hardly ever* are. At this point, just *assume that you are **always** wrong*!

Luckily, this is something else that you can fix! It isn't even very hard. All you need to do is listen for those clues I gave you.

Right now, I bet you don't even know what clues I'm talking about, do you?

Be honest now! How else are you ever going to get better?

This is actually hard proof that you are **stupid** and suffer from the Dunning-Kruger Effect! I just gave you the clues and I pointed out that they were there when I said, *"Those are little clues."*

Did you even notice them? They were right in front of you, and your eyes ran right over them. You really are a dimwit!

Another Little Thinking Exercise for You

First, try to remember what clues I'm talking about here.

Could you do it?

I **knew** you would say that!

So, secondly, go back a little bit in the book, it isn't far, and find the lines with the little dots in front of them. Those are the "clues."

Third, I want you to go over those clues several times. You need to be able to remember them. Actually, go ahead and write them on a piece of paper so you can keep them with you all the time. Put them in your wallet or purse. That way you always have them with you until you do memorize them.

Oh, who am I kidding? You'll never find them! Let me just give them to you again! *Don't forget to write them down this time*!

- It's not hard!

- Can't you see it with your own eyes?

- How are you **not** getting this?

- How **stupid** can you be?

- What part *don't* you understand?

(Did you write them down? - Good! Now take a picture of them with your phone!)

And -*Lastly*, just go about your usual way of doing things- BUT start listening carefully for those clues. When someone says any of those phrases to you, I want you to stop and think about what they are talking about.

Try hard to "see" what they mean. Ask yourself, "Is this person trying to tell me something, or show me something?"

You should try to figure it out for yourself first, but then ask your friend to make sure you got it right. If you did, give yourself a big pat on the back!

Keep doing this until it becomes a habit. Maybe at some point, people will even stop saying those things to you.

Something Else to Work on

If you really want people to stop thinking you're stupid, then you also need to stop arguing when you are *clearly* wrong - AND remember, that *is going to be* **all the time**.

This may be one of the hardest parts of learning how to not be an idiot.

Up until now, you have lived your life thinking that if you say it, it must be true, right? Well, Now is the time to stop believing that nonsense.

Along with the belief that you are always right, you also have a habit of defending yourself when you are wrong. The more wrong you are about something, the harder you fight to make everyone else believe you. That is just another part of the Dunning-Kruger Effect.

Not arguing with your friends when they try to tell you how incorrect you are is going to make you feel like an alcoholic who's been cut off by the bartender, or worse - like a heroin addict who can't get a fix.

That urge to stand up for your right to be an imbecile is going to be strong! So you have to be stronger!

Your first step to recovery is deeply knowing that you have a problem. The best way I have found to get a hardhead like you to succeed with this part is to make you say it to yourself. So get up right now and go to your mirror, look at yourself, and repeat these words out loud to yourself:

*"You are a stupid idiot. You are always **wrong** about everything. Starting today, you are going to turn that around! When someone says you are wrong, instead of arguing like a moron, you are going to just buck under, listen, and try your best to learn something."*

Ok, now, listen to this next part *carefully*, because I don't want this to be one of those things that goes right over your fat head.

You **must** do this every day; maybe even several times a day at first. Write it down and tape it to your mirror so you can say it yourself first thing in the morning and again when brushing your teeth at night. This way you will remind yourself twice every day that you are a numskull and need to work on getting smarter.

Ok? Got it? Stop and take care of that right now.

Now that that's taken care of, here are some tips for dealing with those cravings to argue when what you *really* need to do is just **shut up**:

- Reward yourself with a treat when you don't try to insist that you are right. Choose something you really like ahead of time, so you can think about the reward while you're fighting the urge to argue.

- Tell your close friends and family that you are trying to stop being stupid, and ask for their help. Ask them to gently remind you that you are trying to quit arguing when you're clearly wrong.

- When you feel the urge to argue, try taking a few deep breaths to clear your head and stay calm.

- If that doesn't work, bite your tongue.

- You can even shove your fist in your mouth if you need to.

- Instead of saying, "I know I'm right," practice saying, "Can you explain it to me?" or "Can you show me?"

Remember, this is like an *addiction* and you are going to slip up, especially at first. Don't be too hard on yourself, but as soon as you notice that you are standing up for one of your dumb ass ideas, just stop and admit that you are wrong. This will make it easier for your friends to see that you are trying. They will be more supportive if they see your efforts.

Are you ready for Step 3? In the next chapter, we'll be going over some annoying things stupid people do. Yes, that *does mean you*, so go to the next chapter and get started.

Step 3: For God's Sake, Stop Doing this Stuff!

I bet even *you've* noticed that stupid people do some of the *most* annoying things. Now that you know you are one of those people, it's time to work on the things you do that drive the rest of us crazy!

Get ready for a lot of instruction in this section, because you thick-headed people have a lot to learn here.

Don't Expect People to Read Your Mind – (*Even as Simple as is!*)

Let me just give you an example of what I'm talking about here:

When I had my last yard sale, a seemingly nice lady came up and asked, "Would you take $50?"

There was nothing in her hand and she wasn't pointing or giving me a clue of what she was interested in, so I just asked, "For what?"

She flipped her hand a bit and said, "That!"

Oooo-K! Still having no idea, I asked, "What are you interested in?"

This time she pointed to the left side of the driveway and again said, "That!"

"Could you narrow it down?" I asked, quite sarcastically.

Can you believe that all she said was, "That, over there"?

I finally just told her to go put her hand on what she wanted, and this dumb ass had the nerve to look at me like *I was the stupid* one!

Do you see what I'm trying to say here?

Nope? *Ok, fine!* I'll spell it out for you.

You know when you point and say "Look-ee! Look-ee! Over there!" but no one can figure out what the hell you're talking about? Maybe you're even pointing, but you're so excited, all you can do is jump up and down and yell "Look-ee!"

Unless someone is running naked down the street with their hair on fire, how is anyone supposed to know what you're pointing at? Especially knowing that you get all excited over just about anything – you could have the same reaction to a squirrel walking on a power line!

Let me show you how to make this better.

(*Here is another great chance to practice thinking*)

If you just keep pointing and only saying "Look Over There!" then how in the world do you expect anyone to know what you are talking about? Unless it's something like a raging fire, a spaceship, or a cow strolling down the street, it *might not* be obvious. "That" could be anything, and "there" could be a lot of places.

Stop here for a minute and try to think of some things you could do to make this better. (*Don't cheat by skipping ahead.*)

———◆O◆———

Now that you've given it some thought, how did your ideas stack up to these suggestions?

- You could *describe* the thing you want them to see - what color is it? Is it big or small? What shape is it?

- You could say *where it is*, like "beside that blue building" or "next to that green car."

- And maybe, *just maybe*, YOU TELL THEM WHAT TO LOOK FOR - like what do you want them to look at? A car? A person? An animal? "*That*" is quite vague!

How did your ideas match up? If you were pretty close, then go ahead and move on. If you were very far off base, then maybe put on your dunce hat and practice thinking some more.

Yea, I know thinking is hard, right? But the *more* you work at it, the better you **might** get.

Stop Touching!

Ok, I get it, people touch each other all time, so what's the big deal?

What I am talking about here is when it's done in the most annoying ways possible. Here is a list of times when you need to keep your *damn* hands to yourself!

- Don't slap people on the back unless they are choking. Fools like you might not realize it, but a greeting that includes a couple of hardy slaps on the back with "Hey buddy, how you doing?" is ridiculous!

- The same goes for your playful arm punches! "That a boy"- Punch! Is not fun and it just makes you look like a simpleton!

- Your elbows are off-limits too! Just because they are pointy, doesn't mean you need to use them to *make a point*!

- No tapping people on the nose either! Do you think it's funny? When you say something like, "Well, aren't you a cutie!" then punctuate it with a finger tap or pinch of the nose you seem like you're talking to a child - adults (and probably kids too) don't like it! Just stop!

- Hugs are OK if they are *wanted* by the other person, but that giant bear hug when you pick the person up off their feet and swing them around should be reserved only for people who *enjoy* having the air squeezed out of them and being tossed around like a rag doll!

- This is an important one - pay close attention - No Hands on Assess! This means bottom pats, pinches, grabs - AND no kicks to the seat of the pants either!

Do you get the point here? I hope so because someone is going to *deck your dumb ass* for this shit someday and maybe *then* you will understand!

Don't Act like an Expert

Stupid people always seem to be the biggest know-it-alls around. Why is that? Maybe we have already covered this to a degree, but here are some instances when you just need to keep your mouth shut!

- When talking to your doctor - The latest internet cure-all is NOT something you need to educate your doctor on. They already know and they know more about it than you! If it's legit, *they will tell you!*

- Why did you even take your car to the mechanic if you already know more about what is causing that "ding-ding" noise than they do? – OH! It might be your *damn blinker!* After your mechanic tells you what is actually wrong with your car, ask him how to use the turn signal!

- Does this sound like you? Your friend tells you about a problem he's having with his computer, and they tell you that they are going to get it fixed. Your first reaction is to say, "Oh don't waste your money on that! Here's all you have to do......" – Now, if you are not a computer repair expert, then don't be telling someone how to fix their computer. The same thing goes for any item that they intend to pay a professional to fix. If you are not an expert, then keep your half-ass repair trick to yourself.

Why *exactly* do you think you know everything about *everything*?

No matter what anybody else talks about, you think you know more than everyone else!

Seriously, I *really do* want to know where *the hell* you got that idea! I'm being serious! *Please tell me!*

Hopefully, you get a general idea here, but just in case, I have a list of other things that you don't need to educate people on:

- Don't tell people how to raise their kids.

- Don't stick your nose into anyone's marriage – yea, just don't.

- Do you think you should tell your neighbor how to make their lawn look great? Well, don't unless yours is the best on the block.

- Fashion advice? Hell no!

- How to lose weight? Only if you have lost

100 pounds yourself.

So, just to be sure that we are very clear, if you do not have a specialized degree, specific training, or a long history of experience with something, then you are not in a position to dictate to anyone else how they should do something. Got it?

In case I have not been *abundently* clear – You don't know **anything**! *You just think you do!*

One More Thing

I almost forgot to mention this one - but if I am really going to do justice to helping you quit being totally stupid and annoying, I have to talk about this"

YOU ARE NOT GOD'S GIFT!

That's right! You are **not** – this goes for the guys *and* gals!

Every person of the opposite sex is not attracted to you. Do not assume that they want to hear your gross flirtations. Stop calling people cutesy names like "princes" or "stud muffin." The non-stop flow of over-the-top compliments is just creepy.

Stop making inappropriate references to what's in your pants. It doesn't matter if you have boy parts, girl parts, or **both kinds**, no one wants to hear about them or have their presence pointed out. And don't be trying to make up reasons for the other person to look at them either - just *gross!*

Learn to take a hint - (here it is, pay attention) - if the other person isn't running into your arms, then don't think they are playing hard-to-get. When they insult you and run away from you, it *actually does mean* they want you to leave them **alone**!

This is just another time you need to accept this, move on, and don't act this way anymore.

Speaking of moving on, let's get to the next step. Here we will be reviewing all of the crazy stuff you do on the road.

Step 4: Learn How to Drive or Stay off the Road

A re you still working on that "blinker" thing, or did you figure it out?

Oh, what am I thinking? Of course, you have not figured it out on your own!

Very well. I'll give you a demonstration. Go out to your vehicle and get in.

I'll wait, but take me with you.

———◆O◆———

Alright – in there?

Go ahead and start it up, but leave it in **park**. This is not a field trip, we aren't *going* anywhere.

Ok, now, see those handle-looking things on each side of your steering wheel? Push one down and see if you hear a sound. If not, try the other one.

Hear that funny sound? **Bingo**! That is your left turn signal. Do that when you are going to turn left.

Push that same handle up if you want to turn right.

Yes, it's that simple. I'm glad we finally got that cleared up for you! Now we need to talk about all the other stupid ass shit you do when you are behind the wheel, so get back out of your vehicle then carry on. Please! I don't want you out driving until we go over some stuff.

Making Turns

No, I'm not still talking about the blinker. If I haven't been able to get that through your head by now, then there is nothing more I can do about it.

4-Way Stops

Let's start with 4-way stops. This is when 2 roads cross and every direction has a stop sign, so everyone has to stop. This is another one of those times when it is NOT *always* your turn, ok?

This one is really going to give you a lot of practice because you get to practice *thinking* and you get to practice *noticing other people* out there on the road, AND you get to practice *paying attention while you're driving!*

The first thing you need to learn about is Stop Signs.

I know you've seen them, but contrary to your personal belief, *those are indeed for you too!* When you see one of those big red signs that have "STOP" written on them, it means you *do have to stop.*

I bet you've never had to worry too much about what happens when you *do stop* at one of those signs, but that's why I'm sharing my vast knowledge with you - to help you out.

I'm going to really stretch your imagination here - just try to picture yourself driving on a side street or country road. Pay attention and look out for stop signs. Now, pretend that you are paying enough attention to *see* one, and you *actually* stop.

Wait! Wait! Hold on, you can't just tap the brake a little and then go back to the gas. You need to sit there for a second. Now you're going to practice that thing where you look in front of you, then look to the left and right.

Do you see any other cars in the intersection? – No? Easy there! Let's go ahead and pretend that you do see someone.

Yes, I know, it's hard for you to imagine but it *really does happen!* You just never bothered to notice anyone else before - but you're going to change that, remember?

So let's just pretend that there is a car to your left. The first thing that you have to do now is to figure out if they got there before you did.

As I sit here right now, I swear, I can literally hear 1000 voices asking, "Well, how am I supposed to know who got here first? It must have been me!"

NO! You are not always first, so just to make you go through the motions in your mind, we are going to say that the other car was there before you. For shits and giggles, let's go ahead and imagine that you were watching the road and even saw the other car get there ahead of you.

That's it - the other car got there first, and so, *they* get to go first. You get to go after them.

That wasn't really so hard, was it? Well, I'm really going to blow your piss ant mind with this one. What happens if there are 3 cars at the intersection?

Wrong! You don't just go. There's a stop sign, you have to stop.

I'm not even going to try to get you to figure it out on your own. Nobody has time for that! So here are the steps:

1. Stop at the sign. (*Yes, every time!*)

2. Look around at the other cars. One of them is probably already going through the intersection.

3. To figure out if you are next, you need to see if the other car is to your left or right. If they are on your right then they go next. If they are on your left then it is your turn.

4. If they are straight ahead of you, then you can both go unless one of you is turning.

(Well, damn! I guess I do have to talk about the blinker again. This right here is why you need to start using it!)

5. The person turning has to wait for the person going straight. (YES! Even if *it's you!*)

6. If there are 4 cars, you do the same thing until it is your turn. Remember, if someone is to your right, they will go, then it will be your turn.

7. Use your blinker if you are turning!

Merging into Traffic

Honestly, I don't know how some people manage to stay alive with the way they drive.

How in the hell do you do it? *Um, must be dumb luck*!

A merge is when you're getting into a stream of traffic, like the highway, or a merge lane at a traffic light that lets you turn right without having to wait for a green light. Yes, I am talking about those places where people are always honking at you and flipping you off.

Here are the things you need to know about merging into traffic:

1. NO, you don't just get to go in front of everyone just because it's a merge lane.

2. You need to turn your head and look where the other cars are, and then figure out how

to get into a gap between cars.

3. Don't just accelerate until the merge lane runs out, then expect everyone to make a space available for you.

4. If you are a slow driver, DO NOT get onto the highway going 30 miles per hour! *(Just stay off the highway altogether!)*

5. Also, don't pull in front of another car and then hit the brakes! No wonder you have dents in your bumper!

Traffic Lights

Oh boy, here's another biggie.

We could put human behavior at red lights into several different categories. Of course, there are the *Normal people* - the ones who are paying attention and watching for the light to turn green so that they can continue down the road. You will be able to recognize some of these people because the impatient ones will let you know that the light is green by laying on the horn.

Everyone else will fall into one of the following categories:

- *The beautiful Miss Mary Kay* - this covers all those ridiculous ladies who specifically count on red lights, as this is their scheduled make-up application time. With the visor down, she is starring intently at the mirror. Her mouth is wide open (because it has to be) while putting on yet another layer of mascara.

- *Mr. I think I'm so Cool* - He's got the radio up and the windows down while looking around at the other cars, nodding his head and thumping the sterling wheel. Of course, he is going to check himself out in the mirror too, just to make sure not a hair is out of place. If Mrs. Mary Kay happens to finish her face in time, he'll give her a wink if he can catch her eye.

- *Gross Guy* - His finger is deep up his nose as he chases that elusive booger - ewe! Don't watch, because you just don't know what he will do with it if he manages to get it out of there.

- *Text Savvy* - this covers the ones who can't stay off their phones for 2 minutes. Their eyes are pointed down, deep in concentration because this very important text can't wait and has to be just right.

So which one are you? If the answer is *Gross Guy* I don't even want to know! Never mind, it doesn't matter anyway. No matter which Red Light Personality Trait you have, you are the idiot making the rest of us wait while you get your head out of your ass. Thankfully, someone is always eager to honk and wake you up.

When the person passes you later on and flips you off for seemingly no reason, just know that you made them wait through another round of the traffic light because you didn't have enough sense to pay attention.

That's the lesson here - PAY ATTENTION - so you know when the light is green and you move your ass when it's your turn.

With that, I think we need to end the driving lessons before I decide to take your license away - you moron! Let's continue on to Step 5.

Step 5: Grow Up Already!

*M*aybe I should have pointed this out sooner.

I wrote this for adults – so I assume you consider yourself a grownup – even if you *refuse to act like it*!

Lucky for you, that's what I'm here for – pointing out all the ways you are *messed up*!

When I started this job, I committed to helping you fix all this dumb crap and start a new, smarter life, so let's get on with it.

Another thing you dumbasses have in common is *childish* immaturity. To overcome your current state of stupidity, you have *really* got to grow up!

For starters, no one thinks it's funny when you hike up your leg and aim that *juicy fart* at your victim... especially if you are on a date.

The "*head under the covers*" fart is **not** impressive either!

Seriously, you are not a 5-year-old!

What's *wrong* with you?

Here's a list of a few other things to stop doing:

- Jiggling your belly fat

- Burping contests

- Throwing firecrackers at people

- Pouting when you don't get your way

- Trying to take a picture up someone's skirt (**yes**, *even if it is only to make sure it's a **real** girl!*)

Now that the simple stuff is out of the way, let's talk about things that need deeper discussion.

Learn to Communicate Like the Grownup You Are

When you are arguing with someone – *oh, but you aren't doing that anymore, right?* – but if you do get into a disagreement, you need to behave like an adult and stop acting like a child.

> Again – the 1000 voices screaming "I don't act like a child!"

YES, you do! So just shut up and listen.

Mature people don't resort to calling someone a "big poopy head" just because they are losing an argument! As a matter of fact, they don't call people names at all. Adults simply state their thoughts or opinions.

When the other person tries to talk, you aren't doing yourself any favors when you plug your ears repeating "Naa-Naa-Naa" either. That's for children and *idiots like you!*

No- that last comment is NOT the same thing.

I didn't call you an idiot just now because losing a disagreement. I didn't even do it to insult you.

I did it because you need to hear the truth. That's the only way you will learn!

Oh, come on! Don't start pouting, you big baby!

I'm moving on – sit there and pout if you like.

So, while we are at it, let's go ahead and talk about how you behave when you're pissed off.

How many holes are in your drywall right now? *How many have you patched?*

Do you still have all 8 of your 8-piece dinner set? *And why is that?*

When was the last time you broke a toe? *What did you kick?*

Just because you are mad, *most likely because you feel stupid*, doesn't mean you get to throw a tantrum like a spoiled brat!

This covers everything from

- Stomping off in a huff

- Throwing something through your window

- Bowing up and showing off those *puny* muscles

- Sweeping everything off your desk

- Jumping in your vehicle to burn rubber as you make your exit

Banging your head against the wall should really be on that list too, *but to **be honest**,* if you are really THAT stupid, then, *go for it*! You deserve the headache!

Here's the solution:

It's simple, really. When you're having a disagreement:

First, remember that you are *always wrong*!

This is going to be true for a while – until you conquer your own stupidity. *Just embrace it!*

Second: You can use all of the same techniques to control yourself that I gave you before. You know, the ones to help you stop arguing when you're being stupid.

Hummm

You're clueless again, aren't you?

Here's what I want you to do: go back to Step 2 and refresh your dimwit mind.

Yes, really.

Go ahead. I'll wait here for you. *Again.*

You back? Great!

After you use 1, some, or all of those little tricks to keep yourself under control, the next thing to do is have an *adult conversation*.

That means that you *actually listen* to the other person talk. You let them tell you *their side* of things.

Then you use those thinking skills to try to *understand* what they are saying.

This is what you really should do next: *just agree*! Because hopefully, you know by now that you are *always wrong*.

I can't count on you to do that, though, can I?

I didn't think so.

Since you won't be ready to admit that you are wrong, then you will need to give your side of the case.

Listen carefully: you need to stay calm, and just state the facts.

None of that B.S. I talked about before – like name calling or getting all fired up and acting like an ass hole!

Go ahead and make yourself look like a moron with whatever nonsense you've got to say. Just say it in a nice, easy tone.

After that – seriously, don't make it any worse. When the other person tells you again that you are just not right, *go ahead and **give in***!

I can't stress this enough – YOU ARE ALWAYS WRONG!

With that, we've reached the end of this 5-Step Course.

But wait! There's more!

I know you need all the help I can possibly give you. So I have added a bonus chapter that is going to help you a lot!

Bonus: Stop Being Gullible

D id you do a lot of Snark hunting when you were a kid?

How many brands of dog food have you tasted in your life?

You always fell for the "pull my finger trick", didn't you?

The next thing that you need to learn is that some of the stupidest people are also really gullible. This means that they easily fall for tricks, without even understanding that they have been fooled. This chapter is going to help you SO much! Please make sure that you have plenty of time set aside to take it nice and slow, and even go back to review the material if needed.

I'm going to talk to you about some of the most common trickery to look out for. This is going to help you at least *seem* less stupid. It's also going to possibly save you money, and embarrassment.

Don't Fall for this Internet Bolonia

Fake Stories

Just because it is posted on FaceBook does NOT make it true! *Aliens landed in Michigan?* Oh, Really? It wasn't on the News, but it was on Facebook, so you share it and tell everyone you see that day about it. That's what you should do, right?

Come on! You seriously can't be that dumb, can you? *(There's a clue!)*

I suppose you can because morons like you do it every day!

I hope that by now, you've gotten better at thinking. Yes, I know it's very hard, but you've been working on it and I'm sure you're getting a little better (*maybe*). Right now I want you to pause and think about this:

If something is true, like Aliens landing in Michigan, then what would *stop* it from being all over the news? And why wouldn't everyone be talking about it? You couldn't have been the one and only person to see it on the internet, right?

Ok, is smoke coming out of your ears yet? I know, this is a tough one, right?

Let me explain it a bit. First, no one else is talking about it because most of us are not completely stupid. That's also why it isn't on the News.

There are people on FaceBook who just like to make outlandish stories up. That's right! They get off on seeing just how many idiots they can get to click on the link. "Why?" you ask. Because they *make money* just by getting you airheads to click "read more."

Yep! Every time you fall for it and click the link, you are putting money in some smarter person's bank. Just like that. To be fair, in addition to the money, I bet they get a laugh at how many dummies will fall for their bullshit story!

Fake Friends

I hate to break it to you, but everyone on FaceBook is not your friend.

That really sexy woman or that totally hot man who just sent you a private message is most likely some scumbag in a foreign country just trying to get your information or money from you. They certainly are not who they claim to be. Hell, that hot chick could be some fat dude with warts on his fingers. You just don't know!

These people will often start with a message that just says "Hi" or "Hi beautiful." You may be flattered, but don't fall for it! Soon they will start asking you where you are from and when is your birthday, and they may want to know about your pets or children. Look out for this!

These people may be trying to get enough information so that they can pretend to be you, or they may decide that you are SO gullible, that they can get you to send them money. They may try convincing you that they desperately need the money for some crisis they are having. Another way they get money out of you dip-shits is to say they are madly in love and must meet you in person, but they need you to help them with a plane ticket.

Be really honest now - how many flights have you helped pay for? — Oh! You didn't learn after the first one, huh? Too bad.

You must be a nice person – incredibly gullible, but nice.

Bullshit Emails

You have to watch your emails too. These people will come at you from every direction on the internet. Here are a few things to just delete:

●

You did not win the lottery! There is no lottery in the World that just randomly grabs up email addresses just to give the owners millions of dollars - stupid!

- No King or Prince is a long lost relative who you don't know, but somehow left you billions - idiot!

- Most people on TicTok don't really look like that - dunce!

- You are not locked out of your Amazon or bank account - don't click that link - dumb ass!

- One last thing about FaceBook - They do not give a shit about owning your pictures and even if they did posting, "I do not give FaceBook permission to use my photos" is not going to do anything but give the rest of us a chuckle because of how ridiculously dumb you are!

I don't want to confuse you, knowing how easy it is to do. So let me be crystal clear about something. There are a lot of ways that people can try to fool you on the internet. I talked about FaceBook, Tic-Tok, and emails, but these things can happen literally everywhere you go on the internet that allows people to contact you. You always have to be on the lookout.

There are also many ways to trick gullible people in the real world too, but if society hasn't taught you about it by now, then I don't think there is much I can do for you either.

My best advice moving forward is to keep practicing your thinking skills and continue working on paying attention so that you notice more things. Maybe that will help you to not be a gullible victim quite so much.

Conclusion

Don't feel like you are alone in all this. Some of the stupidest people on Earth have the best jobs. I'm talking about CEOs, government officials, and most famous people. These are pretty much the biggest idiots on the planet. The only difference between you and them is their paycheck and the power they hold.

The good news is that someone was thoughtful enough to give you this book so that one day you may be able to overcome being stupid.

Oh?

Did you think that you are done with that already?

I'm sorry, Rome wasn't built in a day. You are going to have to keep working on all the steps in this book for a while before you can completely overcome your idiotic ways.

I'm sorry if that is a disappointment to you, but it just goes to prove how dumb and gullible you truly are.

As I said before, you have to put in the work, but I am sure that you CAN do it (*maybe*) if you keep practicing.

Do you have those notes in your wallet? How about that little self-chat that is supposed to be on your bathroom mirror?

Have you done those things yet?

Do you even have any clue what I'm talking about right now?

I think I can guess your answers, so what you should do is go back to the beginning and start this all over from the beginning. This time go *really slow*. Cover a small section at a time, and then stop to muddle it over a bit. Take some notes.

I'm sure you'll do better next time.

BEST OF
LUCK
YOU
STUPID
IDIOT!

Thank you SO much for reading my book! I hope you had fun!

Independent authors like me, rely on positive reviews to get sales on Amazon.

If you got a laugh out of this book, please consider leaving a review. You can scan the QR code or use the link below.

Scan Me to Leave a Review If you are NOT too STUPID

PRIVACY.FLOWCODE.COM

FLOWCODE

https://a.co/d/iEyWmxZ

This link also works if you want to order a copy or two for your favorite dummy!

References

References

Dunning, D. (2014, 10 27). We Are All Confident Idiots. *Pacific Standard*.

Parrish, S. (2023). *How Not to Be Stupid*. Farnam Street. Retrieved 02 10, 2023, from fs.blog/How -Not-to-be-stupid/